THE SEATTLE PUB

Washington

BY ANN HEINRICHS

Content Adviser: Garry Schalliol, Outreach Services Division, Washington State Historical Society, Tacoma, Washington

Reading Adviser: Dr. Linda D. Labbo, Department of Reading Education, College of Education, The University of Georgia

COMPASS POINT BOOKS ✦ MINNEAPOLIS, MINNESOTA

Compass Point Books
3109 West 50th Street, #115
Minneapolis, MN 55410

Visit Compass Point Books on the Internet at *www.compasspointbooks.com*
or e-mail your request to *custserv@compasspointbooks.com*

On the cover: Wildflower meadow and Tatoosh Range in Mount Rainier National Park

Photographs ©: Corbis/Craig Tuttle, cover, 1; Digital Stock, 3, 8, 37, 41; Photo Network/Mark
Newman, 5; John Elk III, 6, 7, 10, 24, 25, 26, 35, 38 (bottom), 45, 48 (top); Doug Sokell/Visuals
Unlimited, 9; Tom Stack & Associates/Robert Fried, 12; David Falconer, 13, 31, 43, 47; Tom Stack &
Associates/Terry Donnelly, 14, 30; Hulton/Archives by Getty Images, 15, 17, 19; North Wind Picture
Archives, 16, 18, 46; Corbis, 20; Mark E. Gibson/Visuals Unlimited, 21; Robert McCaw, 22, 44
(middle); William Manning/Image Finders, 27, 42; Corbis/Jim Cummins, 28; Corbis/Jay Syverson, 33;
Corbis/Richard Cummins, 36; Corbis/Neil Rabinowitz, 38 (top); William T. Weber/Visuals Unlimited,
40; Robesus, Inc., 43 (state flag); One Mile Up, Inc., 43 (state seal); Derrick Ditchburn/ Visuals
Unlimited, 44 (top); Artville, 44 (bottom).

Editors: E. Russell Primm, Emily J. Dolbear, and Patricia Stockland
Photo Researcher: Marcie C. Spence
Photo Selector: Linda S. Koutris
Designer: The Design Lab
Cartographer: XNR Productions, Inc.

Library of Congress Cataloging-in-Publication Data
Heinrichs, Ann.
   Washington / by Ann Heinrichs.
      p. cm. — (This land is your land)
   Includes bibliographical references (p.) and index.
   ISBN 0-7565-0350-7 (hardcover : alk. paper)
   1. Washington (State)—Juvenile literature. [1. Washington (State)] I. Title. II. Series.
   F891.3.H45 2004
   979.7—dc21   2002155729

Table of Contents

NOTE: In this book, words that are defined in the glossary are in **bold** *the first time they appear in the text.*

Meriwether Lewis and William Clark explored the northwestern United States. In 1805, they reached the Columbia River in Washington. They followed the river to the Pacific Ocean. As Clark said, the men were "much satisfied with their trip, beholding with astonishment the high waves dashing against the rocks and this immense ocean."

Visitors to Washington still view much of the state with "astonishment." It's a land of forested mountains, vast plains, and rugged coasts. Its towering, snowcapped peaks can be seen from miles away.

With its dense forests, Washington is a leading producer of lumber. The state is rich in farm products, too. Waves of golden wheat stretch across the plains. Washington grows more apples than any other state. It is also a leader in modern **industry** and the home of Microsoft computer software. In addition, both Starbucks coffee and Amazon.com started here.

Now let's explore Washington. Like Lewis and Clark, you'll be "much satisfied" with your trip!

▲ Scenic Mount Rainier National Park is just one of many attractions that draw visitors to Washington.

The Hoh River flows through rain forests in the Olympic Mountains.

Washington is one of the Pacific Northwest states. It's located in the northwest corner of the forty-eight contiguous, or connected, states. Canada is to the north, and Oregon is to the south. Idaho lies along its eastern border. Western Washington faces the Pacific Ocean and the waterways that join the Pacific.

Washington's Olympic **Peninsula** extends out toward the Pacific Ocean. The rugged Olympic Mountains cover much of the peninsula, and dense **rain forests** grow along their western slopes.

▲ **Friday Harbor is located on Puget Sound.**

Puget Sound is the waterway between the peninsula and the mainland. Its coast is jagged and has several small **inlets.** Hundreds of islands are scattered through these waters. Most of Washington's people live on the low plains around Puget Sound. Seattle, the largest city, and Olympia, the state capital, are in this region.

▲ Mount Rainier is the highest point in both the Cascade Mountains and the state of Washington.

The Cascade Mountains rise east of the coastal plains. Snow covers the higher peaks all year round. Glaciers, or huge ice sheets, cling to the high mountainsides, too. Mount Rainier is the highest point in the Cascades and in Washington.

Many of the peaks in the Cascades are "sleeping" **volcanoes.** However, they sometimes wake up! Mount Saint

Helens erupted in 1980. It spewed super-hot ash and rock over several miles.

The Columbia Basin, or Columbia **Plateau,** covers central Washington. Many shallow ravines cut through the basin. The Okanogan Highlands rise in the north-east and are part of the Rocky Mountains. In the south are the Blue Moun-tains, which reach into Washington from Oregon. Near the Idaho border is Spokane, the state's second-largest city.

Washington's major river is the mighty Colum-bia River. The Snake, Spo-

▲ Smoke from the eruption of Mount Saint Helens in 1980

kane, and Yakima are three of the rivers that flow into it. In central Washington, the Columbia makes a large curve called the Big Bend. In the south, the river forms much of Washington's border with Oregon. As it cuts through the Cascades, it creates the spectacular Columbia River Gorge and finally empties into the Pacific Ocean.

▲ A view of the Columbia River from Vantage

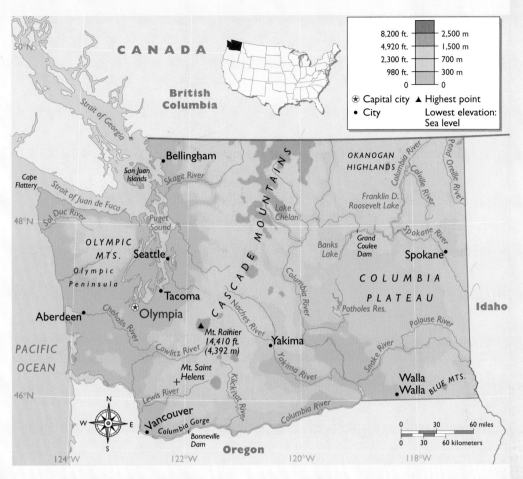

The map shows:
- CANADA
- British Columbia
- 50°N
- Strait of Georgia
- Cape Flattery
- Strait of Juan de Fuca
- San Juan Islands
- Bellingham
- Skagit River
- OKANOGAN HIGHLANDS
- Columbia River
- Colville River
- Pend Oreille River
- 48°N
- Sol Duc River
- Puget Sound
- Lake Chelan
- Franklin D. Roosevelt Lake
- OLYMPIC MTS.
- Olympic Peninsula
- Seattle
- Banks Lake
- Grand Coulee Dam
- Spokane
- Spokane River
- CASCADE MOUNTAINS
- COLUMBIA PLATEAU
- Tacoma
- Columbia River
- Aberdeen
- Olympia
- Chehalis River
- Mt. Rainier 14,410 ft. (4,392 m)
- Naches River
- Potholes Res.
- Palouse River
- Idaho
- PACIFIC OCEAN
- Cowlitz River
- Mt. Saint Helens
- Klickitat River
- Yakima
- Yakima River
- Snake River
- Walla Walla
- BLUE MTS.
- 46°N
- Lewis River
- Vancouver
- Columbia Gorge
- Bonneville Dam
- Columbia River
- Oregon
- 124°W
- 122°W
- 120°W
- 118°W

Map legend:
- 8,200 ft. / 2,500 m
- 4,920 ft. / 1,500 m
- 2,300 ft. / 700 m
- 980 ft. / 300 m
- 0 / 0
- ⊛ Capital city   ▲ Highest point
- • City   Lowest elevation: Sea level

Scale: 0 30 60 miles / 0 30 60 kilometers

▲ **A topographic map of Washington**

The Columbia River is an important source of water-powered electricity. Several dams have been built to harness this energy. Grand Coulee Dam is the largest of them all and forms Franklin D. Roosevelt Lake.

Salmon are abundant in Washington's rivers and streams. These fish spawn, or lay eggs, in the rivers. The

▲ A fish ladder at Rocky Reach Dam

fish that hatch from these eggs **migrate** downstream to the Pacific Ocean. Years later, when it's time for them to spawn, they swim back up the rivers to their original spawning grounds. However, dams make it hard for the salmon to migrate. Engineers attempted several possible solutions to this problem, including "fish ladders" and waterways separate from the dams.

Forests cover more than half the state. Fir, hemlock, and pine trees grow on the mountainsides. They give

Washington its nickname—the Evergreen State. The rain forests of the Olympic Peninsula are like thick jungles.

Bears, deer, elk, beavers, muskrats, and bobcats find shelter in Washington's forests. Pheasant, grouse, and quail live there, too. Waterbirds such as herons, ospreys, ducks, and geese also make their homes in these areas.

Western Washington has a mild climate. However, winter storms sometimes blow in from the North Pacific and bring high winds. Heavy rains fall on the western slopes of the Olympic Mountains and feed the lush forests. The Cascade

▲ A Roosevelt elk in Olympic National Park

Mountains get a large amount of snow in the winter. As a result, roads through the mountains are often closed. East of the Cascades, the climate is much drier. Summers are hotter there, and winters are colder. Much of the Columbia Basin is desertlike. Few trees grow in this area, but desert plants such as sagebrush thrive.

▲ **Snow-covered trees in Snoqualmie National Forest**

A Trip Through Time

Many Native Americans once roamed through Washington's wilderness. The Coast Salish lived around Puget Sound. They fished and gathered clams in the coastal waters. The Chinook lived near the mouth of the Columbia River. They traded dried salmon, canoes, and shells with faraway tribes.

▲ Native Americans caught salmon at Kettle Falls on the Columbia River.

▲ Native American fur trappers in the Pacific Northwest during the early 1800s

The coastal tribes celebrated major events with a potlatch. This was a festival with ceremonial dances and feasting. The host gave out lavish gifts as a sign of his importance. Other tribes in western Washington included the Makah, Nisqually, and Puyallup. They caught salmon, hunted deer, and gathered wild fruits.

Several groups lived east of the Cascades, including the Cayuse, Nez Perce, Okanogan, Spokane, and Yakama. Many of these groups spent the winter in earth lodges by the rivers. During the summer, they made camps in the high meadows. There they hunted and gathered fruit and roots.

Explorers from several nations claimed parts of Washington during the 1700s. Russian fur traders who settled in Alaska in the mid-1700s considered Washington their territory.

Spanish explorers landed near the mouth of the Quinault River in 1775 and claimed that region for Spain.

James Cook of Great Britain sailed up the Washington coast in 1778 and named Cape Flattery. George Vancouver was also from Great Britain and made the same voyage in 1792. He mapped much of the coast and the Puget Sound area. That same year, Robert Gray, an American, sailed into what is now Grays Harbor. He went on to explore the Columbia River and ended up claiming the area for the United States.

In 1803, the U.S. government bought much of what is now the western United States from France. Meriwether

▲ **George Vancouver mapped much of the Washington coast in 1792.**

John Jacob Astor's fur company established Washington's first permanent settlement.

Lewis and William Clark explored these new lands, hoping to find a river route to the Pacific Ocean. In 1805, they reached the ocean by following the Columbia River.

Both British and American traders set up fur trading posts in Washington during the early 1800s. American trader John Jacob Astor's fur company established Fort Okanogan in 1811. It was Washington's first permanent American settlement. British traders for the Hudson's Bay Company opened Fort Vancouver in 1825.

In 1846, the United States and Britain agreed on a boundary between their lands that was set at the 49th parallel. That is the line of **latitude** marking 49 degrees north of the equator. This line still marks Washington's border with the Canadian **province** of British Columbia.

The U.S. Congress created Washington Territory in 1853. As a territory, Washington could officially use U.S. Army troops for protection. This was important because new settlers wanted the Native Americans' lands. Naturally, some Native Americans fought to keep their homeland. However, they were defeated by 1858 and moved to reservations.

Washington became a U.S. state in 1889. By that time, farming, fishing, and logging were major industries. Seattle became an important shipping port, and railroads now connected Washington with America's East Coast. Settlers poured in, and businesses shipped tons of products out.

▲ Two loggers at work near Sequim during the early 1900s

Many Washingtonians lost their jobs during the Great Depression of the 1930s. The federal government tried to improve employment by creating building projects. Thousands of people worked on the Bonneville and Grand Coulee Dams. World War II (1939–1945) also brought more jobs to the state. Washington factories built airplanes, ships, and other war supplies.

After the war, industries expanded faster than ever. More dams were built on the Columbia River. The Boeing Company

▲ **Construction of the Grand Coulee Dam during the 1930s**

▲ **Airplanes at the Boeing Company in Everett**

became a major employer in the Seattle area. Later, Micro-soft and other computer-related industries grew up in this region, too.

Today, the state works hard to keep its industries strong. At the same time, Washington tries to protect its natural treasures—mountains, forests, waters, and wildlife.

In 1997, students at Crestwood Elementary School in Kent were studying the fifty states. They noticed that many had a state insect. However, Washington didn't have one, so the students wrote to their state lawmakers.

The lawmakers responded by asking 25,000 students across the state to vote on an insect for Washington. The winner was the green darner dragonfly. This dragonfly helps Washington's farmers by eating insects that are harmful to crops. After the students made their decision, the lawmakers voted. The dragonfly became the official state insect. The actions of the Crestwood students were an example of government by the people. This is a basic principle of American life.

Washington's state government is organized much like the

▲ **Washington students voted on the green darner dragonfly for their state insect.**

A geopolitical map of Washington

national government. It is divided into three branches—legislative, executive, and judicial. Each branch balances the other two, and the citizens vote to choose their leaders and representatives.

The legislative branch makes the state laws. Washington's voters elect lawmakers to serve in the state legislature. The

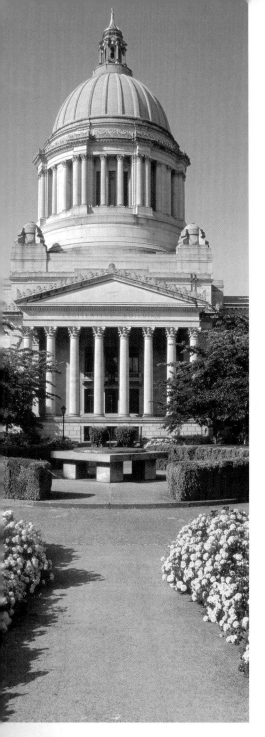

▲ The state capitol
in Olympia

legislature has two houses, or parts. They are the forty-nine-member senate and the ninety-eight-member house of representatives.

The executive branch enforces, or carries out, the state's laws. The governor is the head of the executive branch. Washingtonians vote to choose a governor every four years. They also choose several other important state officials. Part of the governor's job is to appoint hundreds of people to head executive agencies and departments.

The judicial branch is made up of judges and their courts. The judges decide if a law has been broken. Washington's highest court is the state supreme court. It has nine justices, or judges. Every two years, voters elect three of those judges.

On the local level, Washington is divided into thirty-nine counties. Most counties elect a three-member board of commissioners. The commissioners have both legislative and executive duties.

Washington has almost three hundred cities and towns. Cities with at least twenty thousand people may choose home rule. That means they decide on their own form of government. So far, ten cities have chosen home rule. Some elect a mayor or manager and a city council. Others elect commissioners. Most smaller towns elect a mayor and a city council.

▲ Justices who serve on the state supreme court meet in the Temple of Justice in Olympia.

If you like apples, there is a good chance that your favorite comes from Washington. It's the nation's number-one state in apple production. Golden Delicious, Granny Smith, and many other varieties grow there. Washington also ranks first in production of sweet cherries, pears, Concord grapes, red raspberries, and lentils.

Cattle ranches and wheat fields stretch across eastern Washington. Fruit orchards and vegetable farms thrive in the river valleys. Besides apples, Washington produces milk, potatoes, beef cattle, wheat, and hay. Decorative trees and plants are important products, too. They include flower bulbs, shrubs, and

▲ **These different varieties of apples were grown in the Yakima Valley.**

Christmas trees. Peas, onions, asparagus, carrots, and corn are some of the state's vegetable crops.

You are probably familiar with another Washington product—computer software. The gigantic Microsoft Corporation is in Redmond, a suburb of Seattle. Microsoft is the world's biggest software company. Many businesses related to the Internet are located in this area, too.

▲ Crops such as wheat, barley, and canola are grown in these fields in eastern Washington.

▲ A Seattle teacher observes a student writing.

People employed by these companies are called service workers. Instead of selling products, they sell their services. Most Washingtonians hold service jobs. They may work as lawyers, teachers, health care workers, and hotel and restaurant employees.

Look up in the sky, and you might see another Washington product—commercial airplanes! Aircraft are the state's leading factory goods. The Boeing Company makes more passenger airplanes than any other company in the world. Boeing is the state's largest employer. Other Washington factories make ships, computers, and electronics.

Many of Washington's farm products go straight to food-processing plants and are made into flour, cereal, butter, cheese, and canned or frozen foods. Washington's trees are used to make paper and wood products. Only Oregon produces more lumber than Washington.

Washington is one of America's top producers of diatomite, magnesium, and gold. Other valuable state minerals are coal, sand and gravel, crushed stone, portland cement, and gypsum.

Little fishing villages are scattered all along Washington's coast. Both small-scale fishers and huge fishing companies keep busy in the state's waters. They fish in Puget Sound, the northern Pacific Ocean, and the Columbia River. Salmon is the biggest catch. Other fish that are caught include tuna, herring, cod, perch, and flounder. Dungeness crabs are an important catch, too. These large, hard-shelled crabs live only on North America's West Coast.

Foreign trade is important to Washington's economy. Both Seattle and Tacoma are major centers for trade with Asian countries.

▲ **Fishing boats in La Conner Harbor in Skagit County**

Getting to Know Washingtonians

Early settlers traveled to Washington in covered wagons along the Oregon Trail. They came from Missouri and other Midwestern states. Later, immigrants arrived from Canada, Germany, England, Ireland, Sweden, and Norway. Today, about four out of five Washingtonians belong to white **ethnic** groups.

Asians are Washington's largest ethnic **minority.** About one out of twenty residents is Asian American. Many live in the Seattle area, which has strong trade ties with Asia. The state is also home to African-American, Native American, and **Hispanic** people.

Washington has more than twenty Indian reservations. The largest is the Yakama Reservation

▲ **Yakama Indians in native dress at the Indian Culture Center in Toppenish**

in south-central Washington. Other Native American groups include the Kalispel, Spokane, and Makah. The Colville, Lummi, Tulalip, and Muckleshoot Indians also live in Washington.

In 2000, there were 5,894,121 people in Washington. That made it fifteenth in population among the states. Washington grew fast between 1990 and 2000. It gained more than a million people!

About three out of every four residents live in the low-lands around Puget Sound. Seattle is Washington's largest city. Next in size are Spokane, Tacoma, and Vancouver.

Festivals in Washington celebrate the state's history, **cultures,** and natural surroundings. Seattle hosts the Cherry Blossom and Japanese Cultural Festival in April. The city's Northwest Folklife Festival is in May and celebrates the music, dance, and arts of the region's many cultures.

Seattle's Seafair is a big summer event. People enjoy water carnivals and watch boat races. For some, the Milk Carton Derby is the best Seafair attraction. People race in boats made out of empty milk cartons!

▲ A centipede kite at Washington State International Kite Festival

Kite fliers around the world know about Long Beach. The winds in this area make it one of the best kite-flying spots in the world. Every August, Long Beach holds the

International Kite Festival. Rodeos are another state attraction and are held throughout Washington. The biggest one is held in Ellensburg.

Imagine playing softball in snowshoes! That's what happens at Winthrop's International Snowshoe Softball Tournament. Another winter festival is the Great Bavarian Ice Fest in Leavenworth. It features sled-dog races, sleigh rides, and snow sculpting.

Washingtonians enjoy other sports, too. Their baseball champs are the Seattle Mariners. Football fans cheer for the Seattle Seahawks. When basketball season rolls around, the Seattle SuperSonics and the Seattle Storm both take to the court.

Many famous people come from Washington. One is Gary Larson. He draws the unusual *Far Side* cartoons. Another is Bing Crosby, a popular singer from the 1930s through the 1960s. Musicians Kenny Loggins, Jimi Hendrix, and Kenny G were born in Washington. Actors Dyan Cannon, Carol Channing, and Adam West were, too. West played Batman in the original television series.

Let's Explore Washington!

If you want to take a tour of Spokane, board a gondola! This lift takes passengers on a spectacular trip. Hop aboard at Riverfront Park, which is located in the heart of the city. Then you'll ride to the bottom of Spokane Falls and back again.

The Centennial Trail winds for miles along the Spokane River. This nature trail is for hiking or biking only. Along the way, you'll pass marshes where long-legged herons wade. In one area, you'll see ancient Native American rock paintings.

Whitman Mission National Historic Site is near Walla Walla. Marcus and Narcissa Whitman founded a mission there in 1836. Fort Walla Walla

▲ The clock tower in Riverfront Park in Spokane, where you can board a gondola

Museum is a reconstructed pioneer village. Its twenty-two buildings include a schoolhouse, country store, and blacksmith shop. Fort Vancouver National Historic Site is another interesting place to visit. The Hudson's Bay Company had its headquarters here during the 1800s.

Miles of dramatic cliffs and canyons line the Columbia River Gorge. At Grand Coulee Dam you can ride a glass-covered elevator down the front of the dam.

Olympia, the state capital, is at the south end of Puget Sound. Its Capitol Campus includes the state capitol, the hall of justice, and other government buildings. Farther north is Tacoma, home of the huge State History Museum. Tacoma's Fort Nisqually was the first European settlement on Puget Sound. Today, its costumed guides work at their crafts and tell about their daily lives.

▲ **Fort Nisqually at Point Defiance Park**

The tall, pointy Space Needle is Seattle's best-known landmark. People can see this 605-foot (184-meter) tower from miles away. Ride up to the observation deck, where you can look far beyond the city to the ocean and mountains. The nearby Pacific Science Center is full of hands-on science exhibits.

Also be sure to visit Pioneer Square, Seattle's historic district. It contains part of Klondike Gold

▲ **The Space Needle was built for the 1962 Seattle World's Fair.**

Rush National Historic Park. (The rest of the park is located in Alaska.) You'll learn about Alaska's gold rush that occurred during the 1890s and how it affected the area.

Blake Island is located in Puget Sound. Tillicum Village is on the island and explores the culture of Northwestern Native Americans. The San Juan Islands lie farther north and are perfect spots for whale watching.

▲ Tillicum Village is located on Blake Island.

Beaches, sand dunes, and fishing villages line the Pacific Coast. The Makah Museum in Neah Bay preserves artifacts that once belonged to the ancient Makah people. Exhibits include a longhouse, dugout canoes, whaling gear, and carvings. The Lewis and Clark Interpretive Center is near Ilwaco. Its maps and paintings bring the famous expedition to life.

Many nature areas are protected within Washington's national forests and parks. Trek through the unspoiled wilderness of Olympic National Park. You'll pass through high mountain meadows and ancient rain forests where giant trees still grow.

▲ Ruby Beach in Olympic National Park

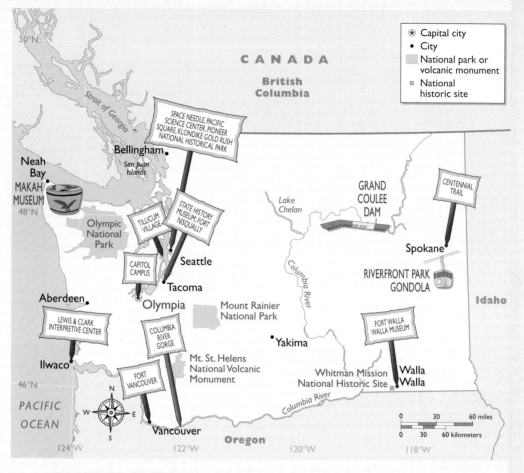

Map labels:

- Capital city
- City
- National park or volcanic monument
- National historic site

CANADA

British Columbia

50°N

Strait of Georgia

SPACE NEEDLE, PACIFIC SCIENCE CENTER, PIONEER SQUARE, KLONDIKE GOLD RUSH NATIONAL HISTORICAL PARK

Bellingham

San Juan Islands

Neah Bay
MAKAH MUSEUM

48°N

Olympic National Park

TILLICUM VILLAGE

STATE HISTORY MUSEUM, FORT NISQUALLY

CAPITOL CAMPUS

Seattle

Tacoma

Aberdeen

Olympia

LEWIS & CLARK INTERPRETIVE CENTER

COLUMBIA RIVER GORGE

Mount Rainier National Park

Lake Chelan

Columbia River

GRAND COULEE DAM

CENTENNIAL TRAIL

Spokane

RIVERFRONT PARK GONDOLA

Idaho

Ilwaco

FORT VANCOUVER

Mt. St. Helens National Volcanic Monument

Yakima

FORT WALLA WALLA MUSEUM

Whitman Mission National Historic Site

Walla Walla

46°N

PACIFIC OCEAN

Vancouver

Oregon

Columbia River

124°W   122°W   120°W   118°W

0   30   60 miles
0   30   60 kilometers

▲ **Places to visit in Washington**

The Cascade Mountains are even more rugged. There you'll gaze upward to jagged peaks and down into deep canyons. Nestled among the northern Cascades is Lake Chelan. High cliffs and dense forests surround this glacier-fed lake. Farther south is the Mount Saint Helens National Volcanic Monument. It preserves thousands of acres damaged

▲ Scenic Chelan Lake is located in the northern Cascade Mountains.

by the 1980 eruption. You can watch films of the awesome event at a center for visitors.

Towering above the snowcapped Cascades is Mount Rainier. Some people call the peak Mount Tacoma—or Tacobet—which is said to be its Native American name meaning "snow-covered peak." Its surrounding national park is full of wildlife, waterfalls, lakes, and glaciers.

Whether you camp, hike, ski, or snowshoe here, you are sure to enjoy the many views offered by this diverse expanse. Washington is a state filled not only with interesting history but also with astonishing natural beauty. You'll agree it's a great place to explore!

Important Dates

1775   Spanish explorers Bruno Heceta and Juan Francisco de la Bodega y Quadra arrive in present-day Washington.

1792   American explorer Robert Gray sails into the Columbia River; George Vancouver of Great Britain maps Washington's coast.

1805   Meriwether Lewis and William Clark reach the Pacific Ocean at the mouth of the Columbia River.

1810   British-Canadian fur traders establish a trading post near Spokane.

1818   Great Britain and the United States jointly occupy the Oregon region, which includes Washington.

1846   Washington's northern border is set at the 49th parallel.

1853   Washington Territory is created.

1855   A gold rush in northeastern Washington brings white settlers and Native Americans into conflict.

1883   The Northern Pacific Railroad links Washington with the East Coast.

1889   Washington becomes the forty-second U.S. state on November 11.

1942   Grand Coulee Dam on the Columbia River is completed.

1962   Seattle holds the Century 21 World's Fair.

1974   Spokane holds the Expo '74 World's Fair.

1980   Mount Saint Helens volcano erupts, causing terrible damage in southwestern Washington.

1996   Gary Locke is elected governor, becoming the first Chinese-American governor in the United States.

Glossary

cultures—groups of people who share beliefs, customs, and a way of life

ethnic—relating to race or nationality

Hispanic—people of Mexican, South American, and other Spanish-speaking cultures

industry—a business or trade

inlets—narrow strips of water running into land from a river, lake, or ocean

latitude—an east-west line around Earth to measure distance from the equator

migrate—to travel to another location

minority—a group making up less than half of the whole

peninsula—a piece of land almost completely surrounded by water

plateau—high, flat land

province—a division of some countries; Canada has ten provinces

rain forests—dense evergreen forests that have heavy rainfall all year

volcanoes—mountains that emit hot gases and melted rock from deep within Earth

Did You Know?

★ Washington is the only state named after a U.S. president.

★ Washington's Rainier Paradise Ranger Station received the heaviest snowfall in North America during one season. Between July 1971 and June 1972, it received 1,122 inches (2,850 cm) of snow fall. That's 93.5 feet (28.5 m)!

★ America's first Father's Day took place on June 19, 1910. Sonora Louise Smart Dodd of Spokane introduced the holiday.

★ Cape Flattery, on Washington's Olympic Peninsula, is the north-westernmost point in the forty-eight contiguous states.

★ Mount Rainier is named after Peter Rainier, a British admiral for the Royal Navy who fought in the Revolutionary War (1775–1783).

State capital: Olympia

State motto: *Al-ki* or *Alki* (Native American word for "bye and bye")

State nickname: Evergreen State

Statehood: November 11, 1889; forty-second state

Land area: 66,582 square miles (172,447 sq km); **rank:** twentieth

Highest point: Mount Rainier, 14,410 feet (4,395 m) above sea level

Lowest point: Sea level along the coast

Highest recorded temperature: 118°F (48°C) in Grant County on July 24, 1928, and at Ice Harbor Dam on August 5, 1961

Lowest recorded temperature: −48°F (−44°C) at Mazama and Winthrop on December 30, 1968

Average January temperature: 30°F (−1°C)

Average July temperature: 66°F (19°C)

Population in 2000: 5,894,121; **rank:** fifteenth

Largest cities in 2000: Seattle (563,374), Spokane (195,629), Tacoma (193,556), Vancouver (143,560)

Factory products: Transportation equipment, computers and other electronics, food products, paper and wood products

Farm products: Timber, beef cattle, milk, apples, wheat

Mining products: Coal, gold, magnesium, sand, gravel

Fishing products: Salmon, cod, flounder, clams, crabs

State flag: Washington's state flag shows the state seal against a field of green. The green stands for Washington's forests.

State seal: The state seal displays a portrait of the first president, George Washington. (The state was named after him.) At the bottom is 1889, the year of Washington's statehood.

State abbreviations: Wash. (traditional); WA (postal)

State Symbols

State bird: American goldfinch or wild canary

State flower: Coast rhododendron

State tree: Western hemlock

State fish: Steelhead trout

State insect: Green darner dragonfly

State fruit: Apple

State grass: Bluebunch wheatgrass

State gem: Petrified wood

State fossil: Columbian mammoth

State dance: Square dance

State ship: *President Washington*

State folk song: "Roll On, Columbia, Roll On"

Making Apple-Yogurt Muffins

A delicious treat made with Washington apples!

Makes twenty-four servings.

INGREDIENTS:

3 cups flour

1 cup sugar

3 1/2 teaspoons baking powder

1/2 teaspoon salt

1/4 teaspoon nutmeg

1 teaspoon cinnamon

3/4 cup margarine

1 cup grated Golden Delicious apples

1 8-ounce carton vanilla yogurt

2 large eggs

DIRECTIONS:

Make sure an adult helps you with the hot oven. Preheat the oven to 350°F. Grease a muffin pan, or line it with paper cups. Mix flour, sugar, baking powder, salt, nutmeg, and cinnamon in a big bowl. Use a fork to mix in margarine until the dough is crumbly. In a separate bowl, mix apples, yogurt, and eggs. Add this to the flour mixture and stir. Spoon into muffin cups, filling each cup about half full. Bake until the muffins spring back when you gently press on the top with a fork (about 20 to 25 minutes).

"Washington, My Home"

Words and music by Helen Davis

This is my country; God gave it to me;
I will protect it, ever keep it free.
Small towns and cities rest here in the sun,
Filled with our laughter, "Thy will be done."

Washington, my home;
Where ever I may roam;
This is my land, my native land,
Washington, my home.
Our verdant forest green,
Caressed by silv'ry stream.
From mountain peak to fields of wheat,
Washington, my home.

There's peace you feel and understand
In this, our own beloved land.
We greet the day with head held high,
And forward ever is our cry.
We'll happy ever be
As people always free.
For you and me a destiny;
Washington my home.

John Jacob Astor (1763–1848) owned the fur company that established Fort Okanogan, Washington's first permanent settlement, in 1811. Astor (pictured above left) was born in Germany and traveled to the United States after the Revolutionary War.

Bob Barker (1923–) hosts the television game show *The Price Is Right.* He was born in Darrington.

Dyan Cannon (1937–) is an actress. She was born Samille Diane Friesen in Tacoma.

Carol Channing (1921–) is an actress and singer. She starred in the musical *Hello, Dolly* (1963). Channing was born in Seattle.

Bing Crosby (1903–1977) was a popular singer and actor from the 1930s through the 1960s. He was born Harry Lillis Crosby in Tacoma.

Kenny G (1956–) is a "smooth jazz" saxophone player. He was born Kenneth Gorelick in Seattle.

Jimi Hendrix (1942–1970) was a rock-and-roll guitarist and composer. He was born James Marshall Hendrix in Seattle.

Robert Joffrey (1930–1988) was a dancer and composer of modern dance. He founded the Joffrey Ballet. Joffrey was born in Seattle.

Chuck Jones (1912–2002) created animated cartoon characters such as Bugs Bunny, Daffy Duck, and Elmer Fudd. Jones was born in Spokane.

Gary Larson (1950–) is the cartoonist who created the *Far Side* cartoons. He was born in Tacoma.

Kenny Loggins (1948–) is a singer and songwriter. Loggins was born in Everett.

Mary McCarthy (1912–1989) wrote novels and short stories. She was born in Seattle.

Dixie Lee Ray (1914–1994) was Washington's first woman governor (1977–1981).

Francis Scobee (1939–1986) was an astronaut born in Cle Elum.

Sealth (1786–1866) was the chief of several Native American tribes in the Puget Sound area. Seattle is named for him.

Smohalla (1815?–1895) was a Wanapum chief and religious leader. Smohalla was born near present-day Walla Walla.

Hillary Swank (1974–) is an Oscar-winning actress. She is from Bellingham.

Adam West (1928–) is an actor who starred in the *Batman* television series. He was born William West Anderson in Walla Walla.

Want to Know More?

At the Library

Cone, Molly, and Sidnee Wheelwright (photographer). *Come Back, Salmon: How a Group of Dedicated Kids Adopted Pigeon Creek and Brought It Back to Life.* San Francisco: Sierra Club Books for Children, 1992.

Furgang, Kathy. *Mount St. Helens: The Smoking Mountain.* New York: PowerKids Press, 2001.

Graf, Mike. *Olympic National Park.* Mankato, Minn.: Bridgestone Books, 2002.

Hoyt-Goldsmith, Diane, and Lawrence Migdale (photographer). *Totem Pole.* New York: Holiday House, 1990.

Luenn, Nancy, and Pierr Morgan (illustrator). *Miser on the Mountain: A Nisqually Legend of Mount Rainier.* Seattle: Sasquatch Books, 1997.

Meeker, Clare Hodgson, and C. J. Casson (photographer). *Lootas Little Wave Eater: An Orphaned Sea Otter's Story.* Seattle: Sasquatch Books, 1999.

Powell, E. Sandy. *Washington.* Minneapolis: Lerner, 2001.

Webster, Christine. *Washington.* Danbury, Conn.: Children's Press, 2003.

On the Web

Access Washington
http://access.wa.gov
To learn about Washington's government and economy

Experience Washington
http://www.tourism.wa.gov
To find out about Washington's events, activities, and sights

Through the Mail

Washington State Capitol
P.O. Box 41000
Olympia, WA 98504
For information on Washington's capitol

Washington State Tourism
Office of Trade and Economic Development
P.O. Box 42500
Olympia, WA 98504
For information on travel and interesting sights in Washington

On the Road

Washington State Capitol
14th and Capitol Way
Olympia, WA 98504
360/586-3460
To visit Washington's state capitol

Index

About the Author

Ann Heinrichs grew up in Fort Smith, Arkansas, and lives in Chicago. She is the author of more than one hundred books for children and young adults on Asian, African, and U.S. history and culture. Ann has also written numerous newspaper, magazine, and encyclopedia articles. She is an award-winning martial artist, specializing in t'ai chi empty-hand and sword forms.

Ann has traveled widely throughout the United States, Africa, Asia, and the Middle East. In exploring each state for this series, she rediscovered the people, history, and resources that make this a great land, as well as the concerns we share with people around the world.